SPECTRUM

POETRY CELEBRATING IDENTITY

SPECTRUM

POETRY CELEBRATING IDENTITY

To Anneline,
creativity breeds
creativity ♡

JJ x

Thank you!

RENARD PRESS

RENARD PRESS LTD

124 City Road
London EC1V 2NX
United Kingdom
info@renardpress.com
020 8050 2928

www.renardpress.com

Spectrum: Poetry Celebrating Identity first published in 2022

Cover design by Will Dady

Printed in the United Kingdom by Severn

ISBN: 978-1-913724-97-9

9 8 7 6 5 4 3 2 1

Renard Press is proud to be a climate positive publisher, removing more carbon from the air than we emit and planting a small forest. For more information see renardpress.com/eco.

CONTENTS

ABOUT SPECTRUM

In February 2021 Renard put out a call for submissions for the New Beginnings poetry project, a competition open to all those who 'felt their voice was silenced in 2020'. We were absolutely overwhelmed by the response to the project, and it became clear how important such projects are in raising the voices of those who feel shut out of the mainstream.

With 2022 has come, for many, a gradual easing of restrictions and an improvement to life – but, of course, for others it has also brought war and oppression, and myriad old prejudices have yet to be banished. How important, then, to celebrate the rich tapestry of the human race, to talk about our differences, to explore others' experiences – and that's exactly what *Spectrum* is: a celebration of identity.

As with any project, there were several vital people working away behind the scenes. Miriam Halahmy, Tom Denbigh, Hannah Fields and Will Dady, the judges, had quite a task whittling down the vast pile of submissions to the shortlist you see here today, and it is testament to their hard work that the list is so varied and rich in talent.

The project was supported by a crowdfunding campaign – thanks in abundance go to all those kind souls who supported the project; their names can be found on p. 163. And finally, our thanks to you, reader, for picking up this book, for supporting this project and, above all, for helping us to celebrate the great spectrum of identity.

THE PUBLISHER

ABOUT THE JUDGES

MIRIAM HALAHMY

Miriam was a teacher for twenty-five years, and, having worked with refugees and asylum seekers in schools, her writing engages with historical and contemporary issues that affect children across time – most notably the plight of refugees. Her young-adult novel, *Hidden*, was a *Sunday Times* Children's Book of the Week, was nominated for the Carnegie Medal and has been adapted for the stage. *Saving Hanno*, Miriam's latest book, is about a boy who comes on the Kindertransport and reflects on the grief and loss experienced by refugee children.

TOM DENBIGH

Tom Denbigh lives in Bristol with an obscene number of books. He is the first Bristol Pride Poet Laureate and a BBC 1Extra Emerging Artist Talent Search winner. He has performed at the Royal Albert Hall and festivals around the UK, and has brought poetry to Brighton and London Prides. He is a producer at Milk Poetry and has facilitated writing workshops for groups of students from the UK and abroad (he is particularly proud of his work with queer young people). His debut collection *...and then she ate him* is out now with Burning Eye Books.

HANNAH FIELDS

Hannah Fields is a writer, editor and publisher from Texas. She founded the independent publishing company,

Folkways Press, in 2020, and launched the company with an anthology, *We Are Not Shadows*, as its inaugural publication. The anthology selected writing from women of all ages and backgrounds and covers a wide range of topics – including issues of race, gender, sexuality, trauma, adversity, disability and more. She has worked on various publications, from children's books to award-winning magazines, along with various publishers in the US and UK.

WILL DADY

Will Dady grew up in the wonderfully named Great Snoring in North Norfolk, and now lives in London. He is the Publisher at Renard Press, which he founded in 2020. A publisher of classic and contemporary fiction, non-fiction, theatre and poetry, part of Renard's raison d'être is to empower and provide a platform to marginalised voices. The New Beginnings project was set up in 2021 as an antidote to the less pleasant aspects of the pandemic, and its huge success in attracting stirring entries has made these projects a firm fixture in Renard's publishing programme.

SPECTRUM

WINNER

GOD IS A TRINI

Rayne Affonso

RUNNER-UP

WHEN I BALANCED WHO I AM UPON
THE TURNING OF A BOOK

Jane Burn

SPECIAL MENTIONS FROM THE JUDGES

MIRIAM HALAHMY

WHALE WATCHING IN THE
ARCTIC CIRCLE

Kerry Ryan

TOM DENBIGH

OLYMPUS

Kat Dixon

HANNAH FIELDS

BARBER OFF THE HARROW ROAD

Jenny Mitchell

WILL DADY

THE BOY FROM THE ESTATE

Steve Baggs

GOD IS A TRINI

Rayne Affonso

sweating bullets in the embassy line, while the older woman in
    front of him
sings praise for her daughter's marriage to a man in Houston
who has one of those computer jobs, she could never remember
    the name,
but their child is bright bright and can't get the valleys out of
    his Yankee trill and

God wishes he didn't wear black when it's so blasted hot,
idly scrolls through Facebook, thumb brushing over the latest
    kidnapping and
the video of that vagrant scratching his balls in the middle of
    Independence Square
and today's Parliament dispute, and God scoffs

at the comments by the party supporters who lie and the party
    supporters
who can stand being lied to, but God himself didn't vote,
because no man with one foot out the door will cut the next one off
if he plans on running and God plans on running, has planned
    on running,

has dreamt of running to a place where sugar doesn't still grow
    in the streets,
bloodied at the root, a place where you can have a girl child

without shittin' bricks, but God still averts his eyes when
his bredrin cuffs down his child mother so hard she has three
    chipped teeth

and God clinked beers with him that day, the dread in his belly not
    unfixable
with some hard local… besides, God is only leaving
to take up temporary residence in his auntie's basement, not really
    his auntie
but the fat sister of his mother's seamstress, whose son he pitched
    marbles with

and God will be back in time for Carnival, to kick his feet up on
    Wednesday
with a buzz from the nostalgia of the present moment's ocean: blue,
as yesterday's devil with her round painted breasts,
as the barrels he will send for his children.

WHEN I BALANCED WHO I AM
UPON THE TURNING OF A BOOK

after Tuesday *by David Wiesner,*
as used in my adult autism assessment

Jane Burn

on this page there are frogs   frogs   frogs
these have been the long waiting years   courage   have courage
you have been learning   who you are   you show the person
    your string   your soft blue handkerchief   your small spoon
so I had to look at all the pages from this book
        Tuesday   the book was called   *Tuesday*   and I said
clock   there's a clock   brightly lit up and the time says   almost nine
there are houses   seen from the roof   another doorway (also lit up)
trees   and on the next page   (said the person doing the assessment)
what is happening   I said my head is very tired   I'm not a baby
        this seems more like a book for babies   I see grass
water   sky   trees with no leaves on them probably   winter or at least
cold   lily pads with frogs   a big moon   a turtle   night-time
lily pads with frogs on them and they are flying   silhouettes of birds
roosting on wires   I do my best to count the frogs   three frogs   four
        frogs   and what looks like three crows flying
five frogs   frogs upside down   a tower with two bright dials
ten frogs flying on lily pads   white painted houses   the frogs
have big plain eyes   man at the table eating bread   milk   white
cupboards   table blender toaster yellow curtains   wall

clock says eleven twenty-one   at the window flying on lily pads   frogs
fourteen frogs and bedsheets   windows houses trees grass clothes line
I'm tired   let's keep going (said the person doing the assessment) frogs
frogs frogs (I think to myself   all fucking frogs)   in a fireplace   old lady
television seen from the back   wires lamp pictures wallpaper armchair
antimacassar glasses hair   what are the frogs doing (said the person
doing the assessment)   (heaven's sake) they are floating on (fucking)
lily pads same as all the other pictures   open doorway   cat   yellow dog
pink tongue frogs red brick chimney   frogs falling off hopping down
a country road going back in the water   three dogs police truck ambulance
blue sky   clouds man squatting   not long now (said the person doing
the assessment)   red barn wall   the shadow of a floating pig
weathercock   a wooden fence   (I'll be thinking frogs for the rest
            of my life)   a big dark roof   a heap of straw
well done (said the person doing the assessment)   I never thought
                    that this is how

                            I'd be defined
I'd rather be made from all the little bits   of all the things I brought
or read   or saw   I choose to be a wheel of time   a wheel of moon
in the sky   the glass wheel of a mild amphibian's eye
                the silver wheel of a spoon's back
                    I choose to be   blue

                                I choose to be

                                    myself.

12 YEARS OLD, IN MY SUPERMAN DRESSING GOWN

Mia Jasmine Rhodes

12 years old, in my Superman dressing gown – the one I liked
    best,
draped around my shoulders, skin sunburnt and swollen,
the knot tied just below my small chest,
resting under the cage holding my thudding heart she had just
    stolen.

Her, standing beyond the thick glass of the Panasonic
    television,
chestnut hair flowing down her spine,
a tool belt resting on her waist, a look of indecision,
buckled under the cage that held both her heart and mine.

I spent that cool August night with my arms thrown around
    my pillow,
beaming into the fabric, flashing my braced teeth, a cage
    around each tooth;
Even my mouth knew I wasn't telling the truth.

My brother, a year younger, but two years more aware,
passes my room on that night of crisp summer air.
I remember the words he said,

the words he left sitting there.

'Are you a lesbian?'

My sunburnt neck began to prickle from the unfamiliar emotion,
as my cheeks dampened, salted like the ocean.
The veil shielding that part of me had been ripped away
in the still darkness, by the boyish silhouette in my doorway.

That word I have since forced myself to love, but at that moment,
at 12 years old, in my Superman dressing gown – the one I
    liked best,
the knot tied just below my small chest,
resting under my stolen, broken heart,
it was the most terrifying word I could have heard.

Mostly because I knew it was true.

A BICYCLE REMINISCES
ABOUT 1962

Far Rockaway, New York, 1981

Ivy Raff

I erode unused, but once I carried the boy over Marine
    Park Bridge on sultry summer,
soirs when Sun Chief sent rays turned whitened rods
    glinting to the surface of me.
I was lightening bolts under the boy's dungarees, and I
    was his joy. His father polished
me, swiped me slick with chemicals to combat the rust.
    Only the best for his boy of few

pleasures and fewer mates at school. Children can be so
    cruel. At PS 102 they lilted
he looked like an alien, plastic cords poking from the
    hearing-box affixed to his thrush-ribbed
chest, sliding into his ear canals, transporting sound from
    speakers along his personal air
waves. On me the boy was king. I held his birdweight,
    quickened in time with his blood,

slowed when he burned ravenous or when August roast
    coaxed the sodium from his skin.
The boy in the cowboy hat and bolo tie. The boy with the
    gap in his gum-tab teeth.
The boy who sopped his mother's borscht and brisket
    drippings with good Jew rye.
The boy who didn't speak a word until his seventh birthday,
    when he tore the shining

gift-bow off my handlebars and set the tip of his tongue to
    the back of his dungeon-
gate teeth and mouthed his first sentence, until then mere
    construct of speech therapy:
Thank You. The boy's voice, untainted by human timbre,
    feathered open. After me, the boy,
bigger, rode other bicycles with rainbows of speeds and
    slimmer tyres, light enough to propel

him quickly through Redfern projects on his way from
    Faber Terrace to the A train. Retired
and reduced to rust, I sighed against the unattached garage,
    and I remembered.

A GARDEN OF NEW SONG

Ewa Gerald Onyebuchi

i'm not sure what it is again, but if it's what they call it,
a body,
then mine is a circuit,
a complex mesh of wires carrying current, running a sketch
through every cell and bone,
draining desires from my soul.
you don't know what you're saying. don't ever ask me to give
    up my demons.
i need them. they put me to sleep, drowning the world's
noise. they sing of a future beyond the sky,
not the one built on maps,
designs made to constrict us,
the flames in our eyes,
to put us in an eclipse of dos and don'ts.
so, you want to know what real sorrow feels like –
grab a knife and cut yourself,
try to chisel out those areas where your
body never quite fits into a home –
a place where birdsongs are tucked behind the night's curtain.
& see pieces moulding up as one, laughing in your face.
this is not an experiment; it's as fickle as the human conscience
that worships grace in a bid to wash off the stains.
each night i wake and look up at the moon
with bloodshot eyes & emotions locked in a cloud of cold light.
but tonight, i will stop my heart from dancing in its electric cage,

my dreams will no longer become bloodstains pulsating in
    an azure of stolen things,
like your milkshake flirting with the tongue of a stranger.

i'll travel through that space where time dies and distance
    becomes past tense;
when I finally awake my body will cease to be a city of
    wreckage and dread,
but a home, whence a garden of new song spins from the
    mouth of birds
learning to live again.

A HIGHLY SENSITIVE MISSION

Lana Silver

When my neighbour's fish died of dehydration, I made excuses,
put my phone on airplane mode. Pointed myself at the clouds –
Were they outside? Dreary as puffy sheep, knowing night-time

like a border collie would soon arrive, blowing
each woolly far away with a lonely, starry howl.
The languid bundles of wool would chew on asteroids,

orbiting old stars, counting with pleasure
how many people could not fall asleep. In a blur,
I unplugged my laptop without shutting it down, waited

like uninteresting mail by my front door,
the company of sad thoughts.
My chubby cheeks were snowballs ready in my clutch.

When I moved to the country, sheep often ran, occasionally kicking.
Hesitating not, entering the mindless evening streets.
I navigated what was left of eyesight or breath – no, both –
I paradoxically stopped for air, after walking for thirty.

My tattered leather boots like a dry felt-tip,
uncomfortably squeaking past the meticulous collage
of white brick. Black iron gates,
hanging fuchsias, a rose leaning weakly out in the yard
– suggesting strangers volunteer water buckets.

After seeing several jet-black cast-iron lamp posts,
making me think of Narnia, I found the entryway.
My eyes held their own – a sharp little flicker.

On arriving, I sprinted under the lavender sky until
I reached the top of Brandon Hill,
where a bench was gratefully stored like yesterday.

I thought it much like the copper coffee canisters
in my grandmother's kitchen, a pillar holding the schedule,
a shadow to her kettle, a thoughtful permanence.

All the flower beds inside were at risk;
if it sparked a harsh rain on interior allotments,
I would strain my eyes to arrange the nearest nature spot,

wishing greatly to be the only one walking around.
I perhaps let my shadow stretch wide over the sward,
unattended by other forms of dark,

wash the clean right out of my heels,
a bath of freshly cut grass.

Ladybirds booking sporadic appointments
with me, in between toes. No warning,
sore digits swimming through the earth.

Bringing them back to life,
scratching them over the cooling lawns,
in my spoilt and sinking state.

Pressing my chin against the calm material
of a bendy paperback, my head lolling
above refreshing emerald,

the wilderness was used to my worries.
squirrels darted against the edges of my shadow,
Their small claws fidgeting with air,
as if flying kites on the wild winds.

My hands floating down my jeans like a sea sponge,
until reaching my knees for a hug.
Offering my watery vision up
to a fish that had no such thing.

I submit my heart to recovery,
night quiets the streets below it like a mother,
little lambs find their trotters again.

The title refers to Elaine N. Aron's *The Highly Sensitive Person: How to Thrive When the World Overwhelms You*.

ALL THAT I AM

Dianne McPhelim

Describe myself? Now or then?
Which one of me would you like to meet?
I am velvet nights and lightning storms
hot tar bubbles popped on country roads
the taste of Welsh mountain streams
and cartwheels on picnic grass
I am the hands that painted violet skies
forgotten songs sang to amber mornings
on furling roads and Tennessee highways
I am the bandaged wing and rising tide
a rusty nail that tore and scarred
the string that tightened as it dried
all the damage they left behind.
I am letters written but never sent
The words I should have said
when the silence grew too loud
I am a whisper above the roar
green shoots among their rubble
the voice that soothed under dollar moons
on bathroom floors, cots, at tables
I am the cool shade of a faraway veranda
Eucalyptus heavy in the air with

just the company of books and birds
that laugh as I trace my name in red dirt

Gather my confetti colours
Wrap them in a cloak and climb
Release, let them fly.

AUTUMN DRIVE WITH FATHER

Sophie Laura Waters

He parks the car and we sit in the front seats parallel
like spies or detectives or the TV couple having
the difficult conversation. Is this cliché
my life now? Is this how I'm made relatable?

So we look out on the leaves which are burning today
in the autumn light and the air crisp as the razor
with which I shaved my chest specially
the night before, to fit the dress I picked;
demure, worn so as to make things clear
but not a challenge to him (he must not feel threatened,
oh let him not feel threatened today oh let him not
admit impediment).

I must give an account of myself.
I give an account of myself.
Who can give an account of herself? I try,
oh I try, and the saying betrays
what's said, the words are not the speaker, I trip and fall
an octave and hear my voice, clear as a knife
cutting close round bare skin in the shower,
itemise me and set out
the evidence: myself.

Here, only my little self,
only this, only me,
take me or leave me, but
please don't leave me like this.
(And worse, I know you don't mean to be leaving, you
     even think this process
is how you stay: so I itemise myself
in order not to lose you.)

Item: a sensitive child
(observe it, just being a child).

Item: clichés about the body.

Item: my sex life (footnote: the humiliation
of telling you this; self-contempt roots
underground in the body's winter but rises in spring
immaculate as a snowdrop).

Item: my poetry converges on images
of clarity and searing winter light and green
blades of grass and bright-red midwinter berries
in thickets of delicate thorns.

Item: two adults having a frank discussion.

Item: you want to be clear
you will not use my name
(not until you're convinced).

Item: a sense of terrific loss
in my life, some disastrous mistake
urgently screaming for correction.

Item: all this could have many causes;
we should not leap to conclusions;
the body of evidence could point to many things;
I point in all directions, a Vitruvian Man.
But. I. Am. Not. A. Man.

Item: I have renamed myself Jane Doe
to better express your grief.

This has been a helpful conversation:
I've said nothing, and you have questioned it.
Of course it is an ongoing process.
There will be more conversations.

We drive back. I get out. Next time,
perhaps, I will not be the passenger.

BACK TO BLACK

after Frank O'Hara, 'The Day Lady Died'

Alyson Smith

It was Saturday, 5.30 p.m.,
when he opened the door of the car,
and I can't remember if it was
cold or warm, but it was bright, and the
early evening sun tainted my view.
It was the day I told him
that sometimes I was a boy,
but mostly I was a girl
and it didn't matter.

I hadn't particularly listened to the news
but knew she had gone.
Gone alone and…
and I thought of my
future I was muddling,
but still it was a future
within the whisper of a song.

BARBER OFF
THE HARROW ROAD

Jenny Mitchell

It's close to a black church, on hallowed ground –
ungentrified – no artisans, no pre-loved signs – FOR SALE
nailed to a cross along the narrow street, free
from traffic noise, the rush of crowds. This barber shop
is brightly lit, stained, glass panel in the door, new
coat of paint to hide the scrawl *Black Lives Out!*

Beyond the threshold, icons are worn photographs
placed on the walls with care – black men and boys
gazing up, angelic models with sharp cuts, afros standing
tall – a black power sign or dark, full moons. Rising
from the radio – 'Wholly Holy' sung by Marvin Gaye –
We will claim love – our salvation!

Three red chairs in a row are thrones, three mirrors
smudged, three sinks, hair-flecked. The barber-god is black,
robe white, unhurried walk, pate shining with a halo's glare –
harsh florescent light. He points, imperious, telling me to sit –
not a roaring voice – soft Jamaican lilt.
My head soon in his hands, the ache is gone.

Palms gentle on warm scalp, I feel his breath as mine
until a towel's grabbed, fanned out, draped around my neck.
The world is tilted back. I'm lowered to the sink's smooth edge.
Water flows, hair baptised, hard fingers give a kind massage.
Soap suds are flicked so tenderly,
to keep the sting from eyes.

I cry to feel this calm, but make no sound except to hum
what I recall of Marvin's song, become my prayer –
We should believe in each other. People,
we have got to come together. More
hate crime spills out of the radio as I stand up, feel new
strength in my sharp cut. Each strand has its own spine.

BBC YOUNG DANCER 2022

Daphne Sampson

To start,
and not unexpected,
a young ballerina,
en point
poised
fast pirouettes
seeming so sure of the long line
of her classical tradition.
Diligent practice from three
but open still
to the wide arc of dance forms
that emerged at audition.

     The spectrum in this group on the cusp of their careers,
so rich and broad,
long-fingered hands
open wide
to receive gifts from each other
we watch as each unwraps
new material
to use, muse, to dream on.
     All searching to make their authentic mark,
find their identity.
A contemporary dancer mimes
shedding a false snake's skin

using the ground, the floor as partner,
not floored
    by the challenges.
    The Round House stage a giant zoetrope,
    the young dancers resist
    the flashy bewitchment of purely technical spin.

     Then Kali holds the stage spellbound,
     strong woman
     stepping out from the Bharatanatyam
     temple dances of South Asia.
     Power, cool and unexpected,
     like a Himalayan glacier
I stand amazed as on that snowy slope.

Followed by a tap-dancing Welsh boy.
He may come close but don't,   don't,   don't
step on his blue patent shoes.
Another unfolds long black limbs,
a street dancer
whose style grew from both popping and hip hop.
Coming closer
to the tap dancer, both giving and taking,

No furled umbrellas
or top hats
here.
    His own clothing provides the perfect dance prop –
a bright scarlet hoodie.

    Could a street dancer take from the tap tradition?
Could he?

Now Mya propels her wheelchair
powerfully on to the disc of stage,
shoulders humping and pumping,
looming up like a young archangel's burgeoning wing nodes.
Face full of joy,
here first and foremost a dancer,
not the disabled one.

Robert moves towards her,
throwing his body across her chair.
Together they become a
newly moulted creature,
spinning the exoskeletal structure
like a discarded carapace.
Then he is on his feet, so she can leap into his lift.
My heart leaves the ground too, into the air
above my own wheelchair
at this choreographic embrace.

BE CAREFUL WHO YOU INVITE HOME

Thea Smiley

They might not understand how we live, she said.
But, to me, it was simple. It was all I knew.

The drive was a long track bisected by a railway.
The house was a barn big enough to ride a horse through.

The front door was at the back and opened into the hall.
The back door was at the front and led into the kitchen.

There were no locks on the doors and we cooked on coal.
My parents slept on a mattress up a ladder in the attic.

My bedroom was an old pigsty beside a concrete yard.
A trapeze hung from a beam and we put on shows.

The loo was in the back garden to one side of the barn.
It was flushed with a bucket hauled out of a pond.

The goat shed was a room at the end of the dairy.
The dairy was a workshop where the crew fused fireworks.

The fireworks were test-fired in the garden or chicken yard.
The chickens laid eggs on straw bales in the garage.

The workshop was where we kept an old record player.
The bathroom was wherever we put the tin bath.

The tin bath was a boat we paddled around the pond.
The pond was so enormous it could've been a lake.

And yes, once, I invited some friends home from school,
and it's true, she was right, they didn't understand.

BODY

after Julia Webb, 'Spilling'

Rachel Burns

you are a broken temple
body, if you were a horse, they'd send you
to the knacker's yard
turn your bones into glue
NO, scratch that
body, you are body standing
under the temple waiting
for the sky to fall
body, you are a human leucocyte antigen B27 positive
body on the track
body as a car crash
body crouched on the starting line
waiting for the firing pistol
body, you are a gun to my head
a game of Russian roulette
click, click, whirr
see how you run
run, rabbit, run
body, you are a broken record
a needle stuck on 'Behind Blue Eyes'
nobody knows what's it like
body, you are a list

of auto-immune problems
as long as my arm
NO, longer than that
body, you are mistake after mistake
a blood-sucking parasite
body, I love you
but I can't live like this
body, body, body
I'm through.

BUT WHERE
ARE YOU REALLY FROM?

Neshma

PART I

Throughout the lands,
Ivory men, omnipresent,
carved from the tusks
of foreseeable extinction.
As our children ask why
the Ivory men's tusks
protrude from their crown.

They warned us of
an earthquake,
which unhinged
the ones with
no stable connection.

For all the Ivory men,
although weak in matter,
had fastened their ropes
on to the land of hopes.

Will you invade my oily teenage skin,
or, against all laws, mute us
so our bristled arm hair
rises to your coercive command?

Or maybe nod and smile,
as we savagely tell you about
the disfigurement of our bodies,
whilst you figure out which
bodies of water to defile.

We could talk,
speak, reveal, express,
until our tongues fall
out of our mouths,

while they remain
in their Ivory Tower.

PART II

There is a string
that tugs me back,
braided so tightly,
bruising my heart.

I unthread my heart
to set it into their stone.
Pursuing the hook,
evading my cage of bone.
As I finally prepare to
hook the string of my heart
on to the unfamiliar lands.

He, a phantasm of
an arrogant form,
approaches me with
his well-kempt Ivory hair.

His veiny foot
sweeps the sand,
which veiled the string
on the land,
now scattered,
hazing my vision.
And – gone! My sight!
Impaled by a harpoon –
my own heart hook.

I had no time to think,
for the earthquake
that shook the lake
had already commenced.

The first wave was only minor.
Nevertheless, the hook
jammed itself deeper,
amidst the intricate
web of my eye's fibre,
constructed by an
ingrained neural spider.

Synchronous with the
pulse of the earth's tremor,
the wilful metal claw
impaled a surgical puncture.

My own metal thorn quarrelled
with my optical aperture.
Frolicking, nonchalantly,
in the labyrinth of my vision.

The hook attempted to
peck the front of my brain –
its nerve!

I knew I had to take it out, for
we dared not to be blinded by anger.

PART III

I sat there with my mother,
grasping the blooded hook.
Many waves came after,
but none hurt more than
the chain of blood
linking my eye to the drain.

Nesma, Heavenly Breeze,
but it seems there is
an absence of breath
in this abundance of air.

Every time I walk
into my house,
the furniture shifts,
changes, moves.
Although hardly noticeable,
it feels unfamiliar.

The benevolent act of
opening your door
is sticking a plaster
over a gushing wound
of your own making.

He taps me on the shoulder,
he demands to know where
my own front door is. I stumble.

'But where are you really from?'
I just came from the shops.

CARDIOGRAM VARIATIONS

Oz Hardwick

The problem was my heart, which had been drawn by a child. So, while both left and right ventricles were plump and strong, red as fire engines, the functional details were entirely absent. Atrioventricular valves? Nowhere to be found. Semilunar valves? Not a sign. Chordae tendineae? Forget it. Look, said the surgeon to his serious students, attentive as crows, each with a shiny clipboard and a pen with the name of the big, swanky hospital. He held my heart high between latex digits, flourishing it like a flag or a sparkler at a New Year's shindig. Who can tell me what's wrong here? The serious students scratched with their pens and avoided eye contact. They were there to learn, not to hazard wild guesses, and they suspected that a single faux pas now would mean a lifetime of humiliation in the places where famous surgeons hung out. Then I, whom everyone had forgotten, laid out on the table like an all-you-can-eat buffet gone cold, cleared my throat and spoke: 'I have wandered the world for sixty winters, with stout legs and a head full of clattering shutters and carrier pigeons. I have welded birds from scrap metal and the songs my grandfather taught me, and I have stacked library shelves with billboards and broken picture frames. I have scraped the silver from mirrors to fashion new eyes and plucked the ribs from my chest to build a ladder to the moon. And although my heart was drawn by a boy of four or five years old, who copied it from a supermarket Valentine, my love is still love, my tears are still tears, and my compassion is an engine pulling homeless souls through a mountain pass at midnight.' Silence settled on the ward, then on the hospital, then on the whole town. For all I know, the entire world may have stopped what it was doing.

CHANGING STATE

Jess Skyleson

I could not identify the moment
we passed the critical point,
only that, by the time I saw them,
it was already too late:

by then I could feel their breath
solidifying around me,
could hear their voices tighten
into invisible bands, trapping me

within walls that appeared out of thin air,
like hoar-frost suddenly snapping
on to a green leaf, its delicate veins gripped
beneath their icy stares,

and under this pressure I knew my heart,
already turned to ice, would surely float.
But it was the fire
that finally touched my skin, each cell exploding

into sublime heat, as my frozen body,
a lit match, transformed
instantaneously into air.
And so now I breathe in,

trying to hold my heart in my lungs, as I feel
the spit from their lips
burning *witch*
into my skin like a brand,

and sense the air, heavy with memories,
condense around me:
becoming water, the only thing
that can never drown.

COMMUNITY PAYBACK

Damon Young

Crossing the Forbury, that pleasure garden
that has long nestled near Reading Gaol,
on my way to hear *De profundis* float around
the clanging corridors in which it was formed,

I saw a group of men with a supervisor nearby.
The sunshine was playful and warming
and their task looked pleasant: the bristling-away
of petals, the pulling of rogue stems from flower beds.

One man turned and I saw
'Community Payback'
across his high-vis vest.

Prisoner C33 picked apart rope
for oakum with starched upper-finger
joints and blood-streaked cuticles.

The contrast in the labour was clear,
but I blanched at this forced display
of shame, this twenty-first century
echo of Clapham Junction disdain.

I listened to that most famous
prisoner's words, and later was drifting
back across the same town-centre patch
of green and bloom as the sun
was softening to nothing.

I felt that I could hear C33 exhorting
the gardening men, telling them
that if the Crown insists on emblazoning their backs,
then they should wear their high-vis vests
like a king wears purple.

DANCE OF THE DRAG QUEENS

Cameron Rew

I do not cry.
I am not a six-foot man.
I'm an inch of raging flame,
with pain much larger than I am,
that wants no fame.

The sight of Scab-Legged Lin,
fingers in the bins at the back of the house,
rummaging for Tuesday's scouse,
reminded me of that dealer's car,
speeding through Vauxhall.

Leering crack-toothed lord pointed, pointing
the side of a lovingly gleaming switchblade
rimmed with crystalline Mcat.
       – Speed bumps clang like spades,
evade blue lights, on into the life of the night.

'Into The Nightlife' – Cyndi Lauper's greatest song.
Throngs in Gbar spinnin', poppers down your chin.
Lit ciggy in your gin, tights swirled up your arse.
Farcical rented boots, women's size six.
Lady Seanne with a stick, cracking the toilet door:
    'any sniffs?!'

Lads bumming biffs, asking you back to kitchens.
Over the water out of your mind; dirty trainers, mucky blinds.
The Birkenhell terrace smelt like old meat and ash.
Beaked up Terry, face like a robber's dog, waving an axe
so you couldn't sit back, even if the cakes of fur didn't make
    you itch.
At least in a ditch you'd see the stars.

I'm an inch of raging flame,
with pain much larger than I am,
that roars our name.

DISSIMILARITIES

Peter Hill

Look at me carefully;
Tell me what you see.
Differentiate if you can
Between you and me

Look as closely as you like,
Try as hard as you can;
What lies upon the surface
Defines not the whole man.

For invisible differences
That you cannot count, nor see,
Are what makes you uniquely you
And me uniquely me.

So should you look at me and judge,
Categorise or label who you see,
Truth is who you thought you saw
Were only glimpses of me.

ELDERLY SWIMMERS AT THE POOL

Cathy Bryant

Light and water have got married,
and we're dancing at the reception.
A stately dance. Splints and sticks
are shut in lockers, while we become
whales and manatees, shimmying
through liquid aquamarine as if
this isn't a miracle.

Even Government departments can't
decide how far we're allowed to swim.
I'm a splashy plodder, arms and legs
doing the little they can.
We're gently slow, most of us,
except the swordfish man, who loves
to slice the pool in half, making
little foamy sexy cuts.

Light and water. Particle and wave.
The peaks and ripples of the waves
refract the light into a concentrated
pattern on the bottom of the pool.
One of those kindly scientific magics.

We are aglow with it, we are run-on
sentences, we are shining and unstoppable.
Age and disability are just words.
We are love, marriage, celebration, eternity,
we the deep dwellers of light and water,
unafraid of time.

EMIGRANT / IMMIGRANT

Roisín Harkin

My parents would tell me
How lucky I am to live such a full life here now,
Where before they lived as shadows,
Nursing the sick, building the roads,
Invisible to those they served,
Yet their accent, hairstyles, fashions,
Shrill markers of their foreignness.

I walk these crooked pavements
Down the street they once lived, passed the mosque
And the boarded-up pub where phantoms
Of my ancestors can be heard lamenting for home,
By the unkempt park where our oldest siblings wobbled
On choppers and played British Bulldog.
It's unrecognisable to them now, this place;
A home that was never home to them,
But, returning a generation later,
Has become one to me.

GROUNDED

Ellie Herda-Grimwood

Some people say the city is intense and far too loud.
I'm not sure I agree with this – instead it makes me proud
to live amongst such noise, where I'm allowed
to stand my ground against my ears,
that keep me down and fuel my fears,
when piercing sounds bring me to tears,
and always have, for years and years.

Mi-so-pho-ni-a is the name
of the condition that threatens
to forever bring me shame, where I succumb –
to anger and sadness without aim,
and give in to the triggers and responses it inflames.

When I'm in the city, though, I feel a sense of calm.
The sounds that push against my ears are like a soothing balm
to this affliction that I can't control
and has, since Time, taken its toll,
but when through city streets I stroll,
I'm lifted up, so sings my soul.

The idling of a bus engine offers a sort of charm;
I worry not about the traffic or the car alarms.
A singing man with his guitar,

the laughter loud from pubs and bars –
with all of this I have no qualms;
my ears feel strong, in no way harmed.

The pfffft of a cyclist whizzing by,
builders shout up high, a baby cries,
feathery sighs as pigeons fly to the sky
and I feel grounded;
my disorder so openly scandalously defied.

For me personally, the city's a welcome cacophony.
A jingle and jangle for my ears to untangle,
clamour and clatter where misophonia doesn't matter.
Instead, the hustle and bustle attempts to tussle
with my ears (so fussy) and up appears
a wall of sound to which I adhere and calm right down,
with the noise and blast and commotion abound.

As my condition worsens with life's general humdrum,
up rise the city sounds, as all encompassing they thrum,
and instead I feel brave, as my ears behave,
obediently tuning in to the alleviating audible waves.

HALF-LIFE

Jazz McCoull

My friend feels the ticking of the clock at his back,
urging him into a future he's never wanted,
and stalls it.
'Japan. America. Amsterdam. Let's go everywhere.'
Let's go anywhere.
There is so much world,
and so small a life to fill it with.

His life is running out
faster than he can catch it,
and mine –
hasn't started. A quarter of a century
with the wrong fucking name.
One day I will mourn the girl who was Jasmine,
and understand how complicated grief can get. One
    day I will tell my mother
that her son was never born. She wanted a boy, rosy-
    cheeked and happy, and got
a half-child with a half-life
measured in minutes,
decaying in its own hands.

More than anything, Jasmine doesn't want
to be ugly. More than anything, she doesn't want
to live and die in a bag of meat

that no amount
of eyeliner and loose dresses
could ever make her own. More than anything
she wants someone,
anyone,
everyone
to tear through her skin
and pull out the person stuck in there,
who cries for help
in her captor's voice.

There is so much world.
I want to devour it, fill myself to bursting,
feel hot rain wash me clean on the shores of the Pacific,
watch radiation dancing in Boreal skies.
I want to take it all hand over fist,
and I cannot reach
further than my skin.

HE

Frankie Whiting

The curled and curved
cartoon flame placed on
its head seems out of place.

Entirely too big for its stem,
the phoenix flower blooms
for just a week.

And I looked at you
that summer,
with your hair shaved off,
yellow dungarees

the exact colour
of the flecks
that adorn the petals.
Your smile mirrored

that of the phoenix.
New but old, aged with wrinkles,
curved indents and dimples
the shape of beaks.

HOME IS HERE

Overcomer Ibiteye

i. in between the jabs and punches and safety of shadows, i explain to my kids how dreams shine better when broken like communion bread. i teach them to recite the Kyrie eleison over and over again because i was taught that life and death are in the power of the tongue and when they point out that my tongue and the rest of my body are antonyms i reply that a body is meant to be marooned in sizzling contradictions – what is a body if not a blancmange of errors?

ii. i know how the sky can be when it holds the sun for too long. i am aware of how longer days can bring danger & i am aware the longer i'm awake the harder my bones fall like failed origami, like pyrex against concrete & i am aware that hope is a swirling bubble that breaks on water, on grief, on bones whose owners fled from their bodies & i am aware that my country is a cocktail of flags and honour stained with blood. my kids ask me why my French tastes like burnt pies, why my Spanish hides my tongue in holes, why people look at us like we were deported from venus. they ask me where my identity is buried and as i try to answer, my throat cells fold into extinction. how do you describe the anatomy of loss to a child? this sacred space where our histories are stored before decaying into stuffy libraries, do you call it a tomb? and this compressed air of happiness sucked into a void, do you call it the future?

iii. but i explain that home is a chaff of radio waves, a TV ad. and in the explanation, there is an underlying anger frosted with helplessness. i explain that home is an album of laughs wrapped in white and black. home is the queue at the country's border. home is a duffel bag of tears and trash. home is a stigma of stars dripping with ash. and sometimes, home is right here, a falling castle wedged between foreign languages.

iv. but they laugh. and in the laughter, there is a whiff of innocence that makes me smile. they recite quotes from black legends; people who bore Africa on their shoulders. they talk about a future bathed in colours, one in which home is an unruffled attire sewn by hands both black and white. i smile again.

I AM NOT WHAT YOU THINK

Jennifer Cousins

I am not what you think.
You see a threat in worn trainers
and a hoodie.
A man who will steal your job,
who will cost you more,
who will use up your houses.

But I am not what you think.

On swollen feet
I walked half of Africa.
Men with greedy eyes
passed me from border to border
for money.
Each day I did not die
was a gift.

I came on a plane
clutching papers, sweating;
scared that the man in the kiosk would say 'No'.

I came on a raft unfit for the sea.
There were many of us at the start,
but not at the end.

I came in a lorry, silent with fear,
surrounded by ice: I was cold.
Some were too cold.

And so I am here,
and I am not what you think.
I am a doctor, a carpenter, a mechanic.
I know how to build, to cook, to teach.
I am a husband, a father, a son.

I am more than what you think I am.

IN SHAA ALLAH

after Danusha Laméris

Fadairo Tesleem

As a child, I grew up learning the craft of
burying one's wants, tribulations & fears

beneath the cool shades of hope. While hope
is another parasitic demon that feeds on its host.

In my religion, *In shaa Allah* means if God wills, a phrase
we've always returned to each time life turns against us.

A mother awaited her martyred son on the same ground
at which fate parted them, In shaa Allah, someday, she

would see her son & again, kiss his forehead.

On this land, peace shall come to stay & nothing would
ever exist to chase it out. The war will be over & we all

shall live to narrate its tales. In shaa Allah, birds would,
again, dance gracefully above our roofs.

May sounds of flutes and drums that connote the emergence
of peace be revived. In shaa Allah, we'll lift the lamp

of solace and may it flutter through edges of our walls.

KEYS TO THE CITY

Deborah Finding

when you bring me to your home town
let's skip the museum of modern art
unless it's to show me the painting
that made you realise you were queer

point out the spot on the hairpin road
where you fell hard from your bike
leaving the scar on your lip that I kissed
and asked about during our first time

lead me to the painted-over alley wall
where the graffiti *fuck the patriarchy*
made you google 'what is patriarchy'
and led you to your first protest march

we can drink coffee in the bookshop
where you discovered Angela Davis
and a cute barista who kept you alert
with caffeine and an uncertain flirtation

kiss me in the rose-scented city park
where you had your first with your first
and again on the street where she left you
alone with a green-inked note of apology

buy me a beer in the ramshackle dive bar
where you came out to your best friends
blind drunk, they stopped you falling then
and you knew after that they always would

I will love you more on every corner
of these autobiographical streets, so open up
my hand and give me the keys to the city
that built you, one beautiful brick at a time

LAVENDER MENACE

Elle Echendu

Somewhere amongst the chaos of my room,
buried deep beneath unread books and partially read class notes,
is a bottle of homemade lavender water.
It sticks out like a sore thumb,
and not just because it's one of the few things
I remember to maintain and refill in my room.
No, it's unusual because it's the sole thing in my room that even
slightly hints at self-care, at any semblance of femininity.

I see my friends eye it with shock
the first time they enter my room,
as if they can't believe that someone as 'function-over-fashion',
chronically forgetful of her own upkeep beyond the bare minimum,
and decidedly unfeminine as me
could own something as delicate as a lavender water.
Even my own mother gave me a strange side-eye
when she saw me standing over the stove,
bag of dried lavender in hand, for the first time.
They should hardly be surprised, really:
lavender has been my favourite flower for as long as I've had one.

Of course,
the benefits of lavender can hardly be understated:
the scent,
the colour,

the view of fields filled with buds rolling gently in the wind,
its almost miraculous calming properties.
I hardly care about any of these (except the calming
properties, on occasion). What really began my love for
lavender happened decades ago, in 1969,
in a seemingly routine meeting for the National Organization
of Women.

At that fateful meeting,
the president of NOW, Betty Friedan,
discussed the threat she thought lesbians
posed to the mainstream feminist movement.
After all, who would want to side with feminists when those
manish, man-hating lesbians
were associated with them?
Lesbians could not be given a platform.
They would draw away from the rest of us.

They were lavender menaces.

In an instant, Friedan lit a fire in lesbians across the nation.
Not only the ones present and alive,
but the little lesbians
like me
in the generations to follow. That simple phrase
lavender menace
sparked a counterprotest lead by
Rita Mae Brown, Karla Jay, Barbara Love, and other iconic
radical feminists.
They disrupted the Second Congress to Unite Women
by entering the meeting inconspicuously

before tearing off their shirts, revealing shirts that read
'I AM A LAVENDER MENACE' underneath.
That counterprotest ended long ago,
and helped successfully bring concerns about
lesbiansism out into mainstream feminist discussions,

but the spirit of the lavender menace lived on.

She lives on in the queer women who dare to love in the only
way how. She lives on in that scared, young girl who isn't sure
if she should look at girls in that way, and she lives on in the
radical, impossible-to-ignore activists rallying in the streets.
She lives on in the young and old, closeted and open, in
every corner of every continent and every place she was told
she couldn't. She lives on in that bottle on my dresser.

So, while buying dried lavender buds,
boiling a fresh batch of water,
and steeping the greying buds
in the rolling water every time the bottle runs out is a pain,
I wouldn't stop doing it for the world.
Because once that bottle is filled to the brim
with the fragrant water and sprayed out into my room,
I am reminded.

I am a lavender menace.

LISTEN, STRANGER MAN

Arinze Chiemenam

Let this poem be a reminder to you that
Black boys are not just grenades of chaos,
Waiting patiently to explode when triggered.

We are not just boxes of metal grief,
Held tightly by tears we were not taught how to shed.
We are more than the stories you've read and heard,
More than the adjectives your mother passed on to you.

We are like the markings on Old Nana's boab tree.
The ones she makes whenever the full moon comes,
While she calls on the earth to bless her farms –
Each with its own curve, each with its own twist.

Yes, we frown – like the boys in your stories, we do.
And when stray dogs bark at our father's daughter
We pick up stones and practice our aiming.

In truth, we have scars, lots of scars –
One on the knee, one on the elbow. A few on the heart.
Yet the smile we wear belongs to us; it is not borrowed –
That's why the sun shines brighter when a black boy smiles.

MEMORY IS A MOTHER TO EVERY LITTLE BEGINNING

Nwuguru Chidiebere Sullivan

I didn't meet my mother at birth; I met her
at six. The day she returned home from
Abakaliki, she crawled into my tongue like a

foreign language, struggling so hard to fit
into syllables sizeable to my mouth. I never
pronounced her well till I was ten. You see,

a mother is only your mother if she was the
morning that unwrapped you to the first touch
of sun. The second time my father forced her

out of our home, I was only six months older
than ten, with frail fingers that were decimal
beggars asking for nothing much but alms from

motherhood. At the eve of her departure, I watched
alongside my elder brother, with eyes inflated with
the arid air of hunger, and I grew into nothing less or

more than a thousand-doored room with
hinges made into fists clenched to young
secrets, the unbeknownst burying their

89

careless hands into my heart, creating a fortress
of pyre that would burn me till I stopped ruing
the morning that refused to open into motherhood.

Remember, born or burn, both begin and end with
an evolution from air particles – dust or ash,
I would later choose to repeat the former at twelve

when my mother would return – to be reborn
through her, to repeat every part of motherhood that
I missed whilst walking into a boy. In all these,

I never talked much about my father, because he was
the constant – a change that was happening to us.
Remember, no matter how clean I try to come with

all these, I can never be more acidic than the truth
that burnt the heart. So I forgive time as if the past
does not spend enough hands to gather future for us.

MOTHER TONGUE

Caroline Am Bergris

Patatas fritas and *chocolate*
were my first words at the age of three –
all a girl needs to survive the world.

My mum was *mamá*, not mum,
but Dad was never *papá* –
he was the monolingual monster that screamed
'This is an English household!
I will not tolerate any other language!'

Mamá was the stubborn scared dragon who breathed,
'As long as I live,
my child will speak Spanish.'

She bombarded me with Colombian songs
and children's poetry to recite on the way home.
English nursery rhymes were just bland,
and English poetry was only what I used in elocution lessons.

I never worried about grammatical mistakes in Spanish,
and blurted out incorrect masculine and feminine nouns
like a steady stream of piss.
But each incorrection in English was agony.

My brain constantly hopscotched between languages,
trying to figure out which best expressed

what I wanted to say.
I hated feelings, but loved *emociónes*.
When I wanted to hurt Mamá I called her 'mother'.

My humour was English: *The Two Ronnies, Yes Minister*,
but my warmth was South American, a baby fireplace.

Mamá gave me an educated Bogotá accent,
which matched my English RP like a pair of earrings,
which soothed my snobbish soul.

I have always chosen laziness over industry,
so as I grew, the surround sound of English
was simply easier. But Mamá refused to answer me
unless I spoke her mother tongue –
the best type of law enforcement,
the best lifelong cultural gift.

Later I learnt French, Latin, Ancient Greek,
German, Egyptian hieroglyphs,
but nothing stuck in the same way.
There are ñs in my soul,
along with *caldo* and *cumbias*,
and delicious swear words –

marica, puta, huevón,
which she denies ever teaching me,
which I absorbed greedily like milk,
which erupt from me still

like primordial lava,
like the Latina that I am.

MUM'S HEELS

Sam Honeybone

An empty house   aged eight or nine
I made my first performance in Mum's leopard-print heels
a bambi-ish re-enactment of learnt femininity   knees buckling
under the weight of this rebirth   begotten from childish curiosity
a disfigured creation of the self.

In the beginning was the Word   And the Word was made Flesh
and that flesh was   dismembered   torn at the limb
in a Bacchic frenzy and sewn back together with queer asymmetry
for Walt to sing of   for Wilfred to mourn over   for Thom to
    make love to.

Could I then be said to be made in God's image?
I who stepped into this body   belonging to my ancestors
its bagginess a sign of my inevitable future
starting with mum's heels   my weapon of choice
constituting my constituent other   the displacement of my self
as I viewed the battlefield that lay between me and the mirror
in a war with an unknown enemy
the unyielding plastic wrapped around my feet
my fortifications of otherness.

MY DEAR IRAQ

Samah Alnuaimi

Beautiful country of the Tigris and Euphrates,
How are you?
Are the precious emerald skies still blue?
It has been a while since I have seen you.
Did you miss me when I left in 2003?
We had to leave for our own safety.

I am the girl who left you because of the war.
My heart beats, hoping to see you again once more.

My dear Iraq
My dear Iraq

I miss your mouth-watering smells of dolma!
I miss my old neighbourhood – people talking, children having fun.

My dear Iraq
My dear Iraq

Red blood spilt because of the war.
White flags waved in surrender, civilians praying for peace.
Evergreen gardens grow.
Empty black oil drums lie lifeless.
Where did it all go wrong?

My dear Iraq
My dear Iraq

I feel lost by myself, surrounded by strangers in a
    new country.
Feelings of misery, I miss being with you.

My dear Iraq.

NEBULOUS STRIKE IN MINNESOTA

Nnadi Samuel

Six months into prepartum trauma, I occupy the alley,
tummy-red and indecent with blood clotting fiercely like
iridescent fog on a Sunday, as I irony my way into a female talk
with my godmother. Her passion for poetry, squeezed
from tonight's sharp want, to cause a small miracle of breeze and
nebulous strike in Minnesota –
whose landscape toughens with maple-wood snow ridden by
the thickest
pang of dust: monsoon flatulence, a gas breaking on my elephant
   feet.
I kegel in the warmth, memorising the old baobab plant potted
   by my foster-
father, whose mortgage
exceeds a headcount and by all means, indebts we – his
   descendants – and
all our afterbears. Loan beyond estimate sits nameless as a
   scattered blood-
right we inherit with caution.
The curse we put a face to, as banks flag down our surname.
   Right here,
taking my godmother
to the moon and back with a love poem, I tongue distance –
   the length of
a metaphor.

Her uplifting to the chorus, desperate for a rising. The way the
    foetus
inside me attains weightlessness,
manly afloat in baritone pulse, the vibe that brings life to rectum.
Tell me about birth, my travelling, my approach to language in
    concealed
weightlessness
of a lost flesh: days I cribbed in my godmother's hut, red clay,
printing its brutal remarks on my turned back, my feet
sashaying the railing my foster-father fixed decades
back, in the timely fashion
of a stone coffin – durable in its wearing out. From the audible
    distance
of a co-wife, the shout fills me with monsoon, ruptured breath,
a daggered flatulence,
released in the harmful custom of a birthing, reeling
the way the foetus folds, clenching its shapeless fist while I
    stabilise my
eager, worn-out breath to suit the calmness of township:
my Iowa dreams, exaggerated everywhere across the border
holding those who raised me. I dragged my skin like an animal
throughout three cardinal points – till my
luck went South. A wanderer, unsettled by the inner works of
    clime,
unable to language in clearly distilled allomorph.
I'm torn apart by grammar, the manner of its safe delivery stuck
between my thighs.
Woman, if not anything, a terror gadget, surviving pills and
    the messy
contractions, to forge a replica from her fallen relic.

Woman, if not anything,
uncontained as the whirlwind. A neat violence, stretched across a
young navel withstanding all harms thrown at it:
the tactics of warfare.

OLYMPUS

Kat Dixon

A woman, streak of blue paint slicing her face –
I put her easily behind the lens, shutter clicks.
She is perfect at this distance. Two men in tutus
bend over, slip on silver canisters. Each street
is rammed with rainbows, flesh. Soho reeks
of history and spilt pints. Beautiful men
hold beautiful men and the sun throws down light
as I pick my way among crowds. This queen,
tiny in fishnets and thong, huge with knowing.
This is her land, conquered, held, ravished, beaten
into a shape she can strut down, glide along, glide inside –
these photographs are painful. Five years on,
kneeling by boxes, flooding that feeling, negatives
of almost-figures, wonders, gods – held up to light.
I must have had an iPhone at that point. Why did I hide?
Thrusting that shutter between me and belonging,
crouching on a corner, changing film. Bodies
swarmed above my eyeline, like a child, like a tourist,
like one who sits on the edge of a motorway,
watching families eat sandwiches at picnic tables,
watching connection, watching from a distance.

ON READING MY TRANSATLANTIC POEM, SHE SENDS ME THE LAUGHING EMOJI

Chiwenite Onyekwelu

& what she means to say is that
my gum blisters.
In every poem where there is

water, there must be pain. The
men stand face-
to-face with erasure – that split

second preceding hyphenation.
That audacity of
the Europeans. Like Narcissus,

a boy black as I am once stood
there, scared & harmless,
until he leapt into the Atlantic &

washed away. They call it suicide;
I say he knew when
to empty the pain. It's another DM

& she says I like the way your
poem cracks open,
all black pain & foggy beginnings.

O lover of my grief – you, too,
want me bent
over on that stinking deck, stripes

on my back. You want them to rise
wide-eyed from
under the snow, walk into my home

& claim my sons. How terribly you
miss the point.
How many more poems before you

understand that history is so sharp
it is a knife
stuck in my chest?

PENANCE

Carolann North

I'm *sorry*

I didn't mean to do it outside your church
                     or in front of your kids
                     or post it online
                     for the world to see

how perverted I am; how brazenly
I walked into Tesco to buy her flowers
for her birthday, held the gerbera tenderly
                     and breathed it in
                     as I once breathed her in
                     by Lake Como.

I didn't mean to daydream
of her laughing
I'm sure you saw the sin all over my face
It's shining out of my eyes

         Father, please forgive me

When I bought her the ring
I made sure it was innocuous; only we can know
                     that blue is the warmest colour
                     that sapphires are a symbol for the
                     heavens

Hidden within a closed circle, pressed tight
against her skin, sleeps
          my heart's inscription
cryptic, poetic, untranslatable

                    the coded message of a sinner.

PINK CARNATIONS OUTSIDE THE RUSSIAN EMBASSY

Tim Kiely

An uneventful morning falls like rain
into a thirsty bed: a lover held
in waking; washing; that place in the lane
where you can have the pastries which you smelt

walking to get the dry-cleaning; hearing
an overplayed radio string quartet.
People have died for hours as nearing
to peace and tedium as these. And yet

their little, unheroic luxury
must still be struggled for. And so we pin
pink flowers on. We hope we will be free
some day to be this dull. A world to win.

PRECIOUS

Suman Gujral

Dad said, let's meet Mum off the bus,
so we left our two rooms in someone else's house,
skipping along, one either side,
small hands in big, warm ones,

laughing, chatting, anticipating the gift
of seeing our mumma, our hair still
tidy from when you had oiled and
plaited it in the dark that morning;

our coats were warm;
we knew we were loved –
this is before we knew we were brown,
when life was Saturdays at the gurdwara,

messing about with our friends, marvelling
at the ladies gossiping and churning out a chapatti
a minute for langar; then sixpence, after,
spent at Woolies, with delicious deliberation;

this is before the world
singed the edges of
our precious souls,
trying to dim our light;

we saw you first, head resting on the window,
eyes closed, weary from the long day;
then you saw us, smiled from all the way inside,
and everything was good.

SAPPHO'S NIGHTWALK

Ozzy Welch

What is love if not the way
I refrain
From kissing her at the bus stop?

She pouts, does not see the vultures waiting;
She has not paid for her ticket yet,
And they are planning,
Asking her if she's had a threesome,
Because she was holding my hand.
God,

What is love but self-restraint?
Begging for her safety whilst I walk home alone,
In protecting her I have forgotten.

I am easy pickings too.

And they are circling
Circling
Circling.

Was she your girlfriend? And
Bet you won't still be gay if I have my way with you. And
Can I turn you? And
I'm going to turn you. And

I lose my footing, and
The vultures are circling, and
They don't stop circling, and

I let them strip the meat from my bare bones –
Crying out would only encourage them more.
I stumble across the cobblestones,
And I text her,
And she says,
I love you more.

SCREW THE PANTOMIME

Jessica Appleby

This world we have made for ourselves is a strange one.

Here's how you play the game –
You need to be smart,
But not overly intelligent – people find that off-putting.
You need to be funny,
But not all the time – people aren't always in the mood to laugh.
You need to be confident,
But for goodness' sake don't be arrogant – self-confidence is
    not in season right now.
You need to be pretty,
But pretty can't be your only thing – flowers wilt over time.

But most of all,

People need to like you.

Just like you. Not love you. Just like.
Just enough, so you can pass by unscathed by ridicule and torment.
Organise the correct opinions
And declutter those unrealistic fantasies of yours.

Can I be honest right now? Is that permitted?
Probably not. Honesty is boring to most.
But here I go.

The pantomime is getting old.

The truth is,
None of this dress-up matters.
Who cares if you're smart, funny, confident or pretty in
    a moderate amount?
People don't matter as much as they think they do.
These pathetic details aren't what matter at all.

Guess what – you should show your intelligence.
If other people can't deal with that,
that's their problem.

If you're funny, make their sides ache –
the world could use a little laughter.
Dare to be confident – know your self-worth and own it.
Be beautiful in a way that doesn't age.

When the dust settles,
It doesn't matter if people like you;
The real question is

Do you like you?

And if not
What are you going to do about it?

SOME COMMENTS ON YOUR THOUGHTS ABOUT BEING BRITISH INDIAN

Anita Goveas

We would like you to not burn your foudni, we would like you to consider which biscuits to dunk, we would like you to find joy in your own skin, we would like you to keep your neckline discreet, we would like you to show your strength silently, we would like you to find your own voice, we would like you to taste the earth in the spices, we would like you to stay calm, we would like you to use condoms, we would like you to learn how to blush, we would like you to wing your eyeliner, we would like you to spell your name again but this time slowly, we would like you to wallow in the sweet perfume of mangoes, we would like you to take the smallest piece, we would like you to be fair and lovely, we would like you to shout at the top of your lungs, we would like you watch Sridevi but not dance like her, we would like you to crave the salt tang of the sea, we would like you to not to want to leave, we would like you to sing sweetly, we would like you to keep your legs covered in church, we would like you to know that the best pomfret don't travel well, we would like you to not need to be beaten, we would like you to learn to say no, we would like you to not mention Winston Churchill, we would like you to learn to be grateful, and to remember all these things at all times, because it is always a test, and you can always do better.

SUNDAY LUNCH

Matt Leonard

I stare at myself in the mirror,
my Sunday best ironed and starched
and my tie choking me with its formality.
Today. Today is the day I tell them.
Oh God, I hate Sunday lunch.

We take our usual pews around the table,
My father, at the head, looming over us from his pulpit.
Taking hands, we all say Grace:
'Forgive me father, for I ~~have~~ am a sinner.'
My father takes up the knife
and carves the sacrificial lamb –
an offering to the ideals of tradition and family.
Potatoes and other vegetables are passed round,
like a reverse collecting plate,
Omniscient eyes ensuring everyone
takes their fair share of greens – even the Brussels sprouts.
This is it. I have to tell them.
Oh God, I hate Sunday lunch.

'Mum, Dad, I'm seeing someone.'
All eyes turn upon me in my time of judgement.
My sisters descend on me and battle
between themselves for the role of High Inquisitor.
'Ooh, I knew it!' 'I knew you looked different!'

'What's her name?' 'What's her name?'
My eyes are fixed firmly on the table,
Afraid to look up.
'His name is Christopher.'
'Christ…' my mother begins,
Finishing before the blasphemy leaves her lips.

A silence falls.
All eyes turn to my father.
He does not speak.
He does not even look at me.
Putting down his fork, he passes his judgement:
'Is he Catholic?'
I nod my head. 'Yes, sir.'

A small nod and he continues eating.
My mother and sisters start speaking again,
and outside a bird joins in the melody,
its dulcet soprano providing the descant
for this Song of Songs.
I look down the table –
maybe there's room for Chris next Sunday lunch.

SUNDAY VAUDEVILLE

Naomi Madlock

As a child contortionist
I would fold myself away
behind the church choir
where lost moths gathered
in the dust.

As a child drag queen
I would lip-synch *glory*
glory hallelujah,
modelling my best
straight face.

As a child thespian
I would tell tales
in the confessional,
for I had committed
no sins.

As a child magician
I would take the eucharist,
palm it, bring my empty
fingers to my mouth
and swallow.

As a child ventriloquist
I would hold the chalice
to my lips, never sip,
and mime:
amen.

SWITCHED OUT

Lucy Zhang

Once your lungs become too contaminated to filter air for the rest of us, you receive a beating heart – just one, strong and unyielding, the way bones click and squeak against one another when they've been screwed on too tightly, stuck in a concrete purgatory, suspended underneath footsteps. A heart is not enough, so you saddle me into a rocket and slam the hatch shut so the spacecraft can dislodge itself and rumble the ground away. In exchange for me, you receive a face – your old one, not the one you wear, now built from plastics and glue. I remember your original face: its eyeballs and organs uselessly capable of thousands of expressions. Textured like it was composed of pebbles I'd pluck. You told me if a single pebble were removed, you'd no longer be you, so I stopped scratching and patiently waited for a pebble to fall away. In the end, your whole face came off, like a mask cut from the bottom of a pot speckled with drainage holes, and we found you a new one with perfect eyes and lips and ears and cheeks, smooth like it'd been coated in tapioca starch and oil. With those eyes, we watch the earth crackle, a sheet of sesame crisp shattering into roast seeds I think can still sprout. You call me dumb. You wave as though you are the one leaving. In exchange for any remaining time, you receive a liver and a kidney and a pair of hands – new and sturdy to hold up the sky long enough for me to leave orbit. The sky crushes you after I've made it to the galaxy. Mountains flatten like pulverised Styrofoam. Oceans ooze from the universe's edges. I imagine rolling it all up: your heart and eyes and limbs studding a sheet of earth the way kumquats and jujubes decorate sticky rice, waiting to be picked off, deconstructed. Because that's how it is – you lose and then reassemble. I wait for you to suck in your intestine, reinflate your crushed deltoids, exchange your squashed heart for whatever you've got left, lift the sky back up so I can return safely.

T4T
(TRANS FOR TRANS)

Abhainn Connolly

I

The night before your first testosterone shot,
your mouth negotiates with the parts of my body
that throw white flags to the world – the traitors. You call
me perfect, & I know exactly who you mean. Tomorrow
I will pinch your thigh & hold the bridge of myself steady
between you & your right blood.

II

The insurance company says I am not trans enough
for my surrender to be anything but cosmetic,
& I cannot afford to be not trans enough. I have looked
into a thousand mirrors & never once felt seen,
my skin a tomb I walk around in, waiting for the air
to run out. I have spent my life digging holes, chosen lovers
for their shovels. When you tell me you'd recognise me anywhere,
I know exactly who you mean.

III

Isn't love so uncertain? It is through this den of
trepidation that we breathe. We create all the right confusion
in the right people. I'm learning how to be
unsure & trusting. I'm learning how to ask
your body who you are every day. Let what is right
enter us & move the muscle & fat from our hips.
Let the surgeons cut smiles into your chest
& under my belly. We will reinvent our bodies.

IV

They'll ask us who we are & the answer will be
that we love each other. We are becoming what we are
& we are what we are all at once. & don't we love it
like that? Don't I love all of you at once?

THE BOY FROM THE ESTATE

Steve Baggs

The boy from the estate is here to see you!
The one who was told at thirteen that his mother
　　would never survive.
The one who didn't join the street gang.
Walked home with a bloodied shirt,
Dodged the blades in late-night alleys.

The boy the politicians dropped through the net.
Having to work zero-hour contracts
To support his apprenticeship.
Ran a marathon to save his brother.
Climbed the stairwells full of needles.

Labelled more than once,
Even though he loved the library.
Avoided drugs and guns.
Wouldn't do the county lines,
But took his wheelchaired dad to the country.

Did all the paperwork,
Even though the benefits were late.
Had to move because of the cladding.
Relocated to a seaside town,
Where his accent gave him away.

The boy from the estate is here to see you!
He knocked that cliché out of town.
Graduated in an Oxford gown.
Head of the company at thirty-nine.
Ended it all on the circle line.

THE COLLECTOR

Jessica Oakwood

First there was the label
of highly sensitive, gently floated by the doctor
across the waters of my delicate mind.
Then a psychiatrist in A&E
suggested Generalised Anxiety Disorder
and Major Depressive Disorder.
These labels, like the discount vouchers
on a book you buy as a gift
cling stubbornly, long after you try
to remove them with a pink
scouring pad and a dab of Fairy liquid.

I wonder if all these labels count as hoarding?
That's another label I could get behind. Disposophobia.
You should see the piles of piles of stuff I am accruing in the
　　　house.
My friend says I have to stop, but I'm not sure how.
Anyway, after GAD and MDD, acronyms are my thing now,
　　　apparently.

Then came Autism. It snuck in there when I wasn't looking;
apparently it had been with me all along,
like a birthmark I'd never noticed.
A different brain. A different operating system.
After that, came psychosis.

A word that's bitty to chew, and changes in texture as you go,
like eating your way through a Fab ice lolly.
Then Schizoaffective Disorder a year later.
Conditions toppling like dominoes.

I used to be defined by my job,
but I don't have one of those any more.
I think my parents had hope I would write a book,
but after ten years whisking up syllables for cash,
I became a full-time mental-health patient.
Being chronically ill is my profession now.
Anyway, I don't think I identified as anything before this
    happened,
I just floated around somewhere between workaholic and
    girlboss,
somewhere between partygirl and alcoholic,
never quite reaching the shelf with the labels on.
Labels are almost a kind of privilege, I've learnt.
Although I hesitate to use that word.
The waiting lists are so long,
the services so underfunded,
that being really, REALLY sick –
so sick they section you against your will –
has become an enviable position to be in,
from the perspective
of finally getting the answers
I've been looking for all these years.

So anyway, I gather up my labels.,
These different facets of my identity.
Some I got from hospitals, some from the doctor's office;

A few I got myself second-hand from Google,
then got them authenticated by the pros.
I'm still trying to find someone to give
me the official seal of approval
for OCD and ADHD.
Not sure why I bother, though.
What difference does it make to me?
As long as I get my meds each month.
These little pills keep me sane(ish).

I notice on my Twitter bio, of all things,
how I feel about my identity, the things I define myself by,
they change day to day.
Some may call them labels, others might call them just
simply
me.

It's not conditions that shape my identity,
but other facets of my experience, too.
For example, I wonder now
if that relationship I had with my best friend at uni
makes me bi or pan – I'm not sure which yet.

Not just that, but
I'm exploring the feeling, or absence, rather, of
gender that I feel;
it's different for others, unique to each of us.
But for me, sometimes, my gender is like a costume I put on
each day.
A demigirl, I think I've settled on, I feel mostly genderless,
but sometimes female.

They have names for all of this,
but no one told me.
I am outside the outside.
It seems to me
that these things are all
spectrums. 3D, 4D, infinitely
sliding scales,
the labels themselves simply a way to make sense of things
that are often nuanced.

So who am I?
What is in my ingredients list? My identity?
Am I a fruit loop? And I say that with affection.
I am a rainbow of colour
in a world of shredded wheats.

I kind of like to think that, rather than labels,
I am on spectrums –
'an anomalous point,' that psychiatrist called me.
I forget which one –
there have been so many.
I am colourful.
Flittering through the dark like static,
the TV left on and the technicolour fuzz cutting into the dark.
Maybe the only label I have is unique to me.
A label for each of us.
Beneath all these hand-scrawled luggage tags,
that are man-made concepts, anyway,
I am just
me.

THE ODD SPACE IN BETWEEN

Raina Muriithi

You can't say you're European
because your hair texture isn't right.
You're bilingual, for goodness' sake,
and what's more is
you're not white.
You don't possess a dainty figure
or share in the conquering history of the empire.
Despite knowing all the facts
about the world wars
you have the wrong nose
and a tongue like fire.

Yet

you can't say you're African,
because you're not able to speak your mother tongue.
You don't understand the conjugal roles,
the decorum or even
the social procedures at family functions.
Your skirt is too short
and you have piercings like a cow.
You don't understand that women speak when spoken to
and when something is said you do it now.

Yet

you do not hesitate to ask if
you have a place in this nothingness
of identity. Of belonging. Of community.

You occupy the odd space in between.

The makeshift peculiarity formed in
the vacuum created by a conquistador legacy.
Though you may never
truly sustain being African
in its bona fide configuration,
you'll never be able to impress
the others with your
cello playing, code switching or hair mutilation.

This undefined space
reminds you you're black
because you're African, but
you will never ever be able to
amount to the status
of being white.

THE WRAITH AND THE MAGPIE

LJ Ireton

The colours leeched out so slowly
I didn't see them seep out.
Ironic, for someone who hyper-fixates
On detail –
But I was on the ground looking for clues,
My disorder the detective's glass,
Looking for anything out of place –
Danger, sticks, risks;
I must fix everything.
My cloak soaked up my colour,
Swallowed its own shadow,
Until I was a wraith, pacing
Pavements.
You were watching, I know:
'Crazy lady.'
But I'm just obsessed with safety –
The kindest kind of heart; surely
It must be even more visible
Through this shadow form –
Veiled thinly,
Glittering a little.
On the better days,
My mind magnifies
The fae flowers and feather sheens,

Glints, tiny good things
No one sees –
I pick them out,
Weave and wave, parade them,
My magpie gifts,
And I am
A solid, colourful shape,
Outlined in glitter.

Inspired by my life with Obsessive Compulsive Disorder.

TO THE CAGED BIRD IN CHURCH

Martins Deep

The front pew is quicksand
whenever your sin is the sermon.

The crow perched on your pastor's shoulder
whispers into his ears.

You grimace as the usher points you
where death row will cast its shadow on your wings,

till it freezes up, and you can only reimagine hellfire
as the only place to thaw it.
These many Sundays, and you're still not good at playing deaf;
your ears shut against arrows poisoned in olive oil to pierce you.

And today, the gravitational pull to the restroom is too weak
to suck you through the back door that leads to the address of
     a rainbow drinker.

And you're praying to a bird pecking at its reflection on the
     stained-glass window,
to pick the lock of this cage beaten every Sunday into another
     layer of your skin.

TRANSFORMATION

Susan Cartwright-Smith

I held you in my arms –
my baby girl.
And in that instant dreamt of weddings,
heart broken by a man,
your own joy, holding future babies of your own.
But as my ends betray, I am not the conditioning kind.
When you cut through your skin,
was it to see the real you beneath?
Slicing through the chrysalis, unravelling the silken story of
    your previous existence.
Your dampened wings became a different creature,
flying high.
A young man grows in your place.
He wears your face, but has been stitched together differently.
And looking at my son, now, different name and different
    contours,
I wonder
what I did
which made you not quite who you were,
who you were meant to be.
Was it me who made the journey different? Made you
    spurn the map
and travel down the overgrown path?

I hold my second son, and wonder:
will he take a different path? Do I produce just boys?

Or just mistakes?

But you are now rubbed out and drawn anew –
my primitive daubing covered over by your masterpiece.
The cave painting, rendered by Picasso, smudged and
    smoothed, presented fresh by Holbein.

A braver hand than mine, touching up, finishing off.
What I see is perfect,
as it was before.

But this is YOU. Who you are. Who you need to be.
And I am full of love for you, daughter no more.

My son.

WHALE WATCHING
IN THE ARCTIC CIRCLE

Kerry Ryan

It has survived pollution, city noise and melting icecaps, you read.
Our cabin by the engine room has no window and a diesel stink,
but we are here. We have made it. The likes of us.
It has survived predation… The look you give me then
would power the northern lights, smash bergs in Baffin Bay.
Old survivor, you whisper when we spoon in bed. *Old friend*.
Each day we ignore your cough, leave the pills in the canvas bag.
On deck, we hold hands like fool teens. Others in thicker coats tut:
only the beluga, the narwhal, but where are the orcas? The killers?
You shrug, snap glaciers, birds, ice-choked channels with your Nokia.
You pause to sip the clean air as if it's kaolin and morphine.
On the last night, you lie with a headache, and I read to you.
The legends say if you die at sea, you will be reborn as an orca.
When I wake, the bed is cold, and outside: a click, a pulse, a splash.

WHERE FOUR WORLDS MEET

Dave Wynne-Jones

I

I remember my daughter in rural Wrexham
bringing her new friend into our garden
to show me her 'Pakistani uniform',
as I go to meet a plane at Islamabad airport
and am asked, 'Do you live here in Pakistan?'
by a guy from Bradford whose brown skin
enables him more easily to blend in,
despite wearing a suit, shirt and tie.
His surprise is seen too in the eyes
of others power-dressing, western-style,
whereas I wear the shalwar kameez,
trying to be cool in this huge heat.

II

Riding a rutted, crumbling jeep track
over the Lowari Pass to Chitral,
through hill country indistinguishable
from Kashmir or Morocco, arid, rugged,
the same terracing, same flat-roofed buildings,
my Berber headgear keeps off the sun,
scarfs against the clouds of choking dust;
a variation on that self-same theme –
adapting to a harsh environment.

III

In a desert of dry stones
we hunt for a glacier,
realising, too late,
how ice-flesh hides
beneath a twitching coat
of dense moraine,
accumulating gravel,
broken rock, slowly,
over centuries,
above this shrinking ice,
like the falling sands
of an hourglass.

IV

All day under a beating sun,
reading the secret language of stone
in slate, granite, quartz and schist,
my feet found their way
like fingers across a page of braille.
At night under the silent stars
I listen to guttural consonants,
staccato plosives answering
the hiss of snowslides,
echoes of other tongues.

V

On a trail to summer grazing near the Afghan border,
passing a few stone and mud-walled dwellings
where a woman and children were herding goats,
a girl approached, clutching a bundle to show us,
lifting the worn, homespun blanket aside
to reveal a baby, haze of red hair, a face
still smeared with afterbirth mucus,
opening bright-blue, unfocused eyes;
a scion of Alexander's stock, perhaps.

VI

Would you recognise this junction now, Fosco?
A Hindu Kush with Hindus in retreat,
Buddhism clinging on in tiny enclaves,
Communism at one remove in China,
and Islam militant.
A Pashtun, a Kalashnikov over his shoulder,
wanders down the path from our base camp,
waves to a shepherd bringing down the flock
to water at a spring amidst the trees.
'Hunter?' 'No, Taliban. They are
the good guys. Kill Russians!' Azim tells me.
We thought so too, in 1999.

The title is a reference to *Where Four Worlds Meet* by Fosco Mariani
(1959), a book about an expedition to the Hindu Kush.

ABOUT THE POETS

RAYNE AFFONSO *p. 17*

Rayne Affonso lives in Trinidad and Tobago, where she is double-majoring in Spanish and English Literature at the University of the West Indies. Her work has been published in *Pilcrow & Dagger*, *The Daphne Review* and *Diverse Voices Quarterly*.

SAMAH ALNUAIMI *p. 95*

Samah Alnuaimi was born in Iraq. Unfortunately, during the Iraq War she had to leave because it was no longer safe. Her family moved to Syria, and from there to England, where they settled in Bradford. Samah credits these experiences as developing her passion for poetry, which became a form of escape, and a way to express herself and clear my mind. She is currently studying to become an interpreter, and hopes to study law, a subject she finds extremely interesting.

CAROLINE AM BERGRIS *p. 91*

Caroline Am Bergris lives in London and loves poached eggs and cheese, but not together. She is mentally and physically disabled, but also considers not living next-door to Waitrose a disability. She struggles with reading, talking and moving, and loves poetry, as it is a more manageable art form for her. She has been published in magazines, journals and anthologies in Europe and America, and has won two poetry competitions. In other lives, she taught medical students sociology, offenders anger management and herself hieroglyphics.

JESSICA APPLEBY *p. 113*

Jessica Appleby was born in England and works as a Learning Support Assistant. She has a passion for writing fantasy novels and poetry. Obsessed with books and singing, she has been previously published in a Busta Rhyme Poetry Competition when she was fifteen.

STEVE BAGGS *p. 125*

Steve Baggs is a poet and writer who was born in Deal in Kent and now lives in Canterbury. He has been published in several poetry magazines and is putting together his first collection of poetry. He has previously won a Co-Op Poetry Festival prize, and has performed his poetry across the country – including when he was once arrested for an impromptu poetry reading as part of a teenage guerrilla poetry night. Thankfully, it was all a misunderstanding! He enjoys writing haiku and has contributed to the *Time Haiku* magazine, and recently won second prize for a haibun he wrote as part of a *Time Haiku* competition. Steve is currently writing a memoir about playing village cricket. He is delighted to be contributing to this excellent poetry anthology.

CATHY BRYANT *p. 65*

After being homeless in her teens, Cathy Bryant worked as a life model, shoe-shop assistant, civil servant and childminder. When she became too disabled to work full-time, Cathy started submitting writing. She now has hundreds of pieces published and three poetry collections, and has won over thirty literary awards. Cathy also runs the Comps and Calls website that lists free opportunities for writers. She lives in Salford, UK, with her partner, who is also a writer.

JANE BURN *p. 19*

Jane Burn is an award-winning, working-class, pan-sexual, autistic poet, artist, parent and essayist. Her essays have appeared in *New Defences of Poetry*, *The Friday Poem*, *Un/Natural Showcase* for D/deaf, disabled and/or neurodivergent nature writers funded by the Royal Society of Literature's *Literature Matters* programme and the Rebecca Swift Foundation. Her poems are widely published, and she has recently brought out a collection, *Be Feared*.

RACHEL BURNS *p. 47*

Rachel Burns lives on the outskirts of Durham. She has a poetry pamphlet in print, *A Girl in a Blue Dress*. She came second in the Julian Lennon Prize for Poetry and was longlisted in the National Poetry Competition 2021.

SUSAN CARTWRIGHT-SMITH *p. 137*

Susan Cartwright-Smith is a writer, workshop leader and illustrator from Carlisle. She has made costumes for Manchester Royal Exchange, English National Opera and ACT Youth Theatre, Carlisle, and fabric illustrations for the Diverse Cumbria finalist exhibition *Mind Trees of the Urban Forest*, which she designed and curated. Being a wild swimmer and fell walker inspires her, and her work has been published in *Cumbria* magazine, as well as in anthologies for Forward Poetry and Arachne Press. She has been the writer in residence for Gosling Sike at Cumbria Wildlife Trust since 2020.

NWUGURU CHIDIEBERE SULLIVAN *p. 89*

Nwuguru Chidiebere Sullivan is a speculative writer of Izzi, Abakaliki ancestry. He is a medical laboratory science student, and his poetry has been nominated for the Forward Prize, the Pushcart Prize and the Best of the Net Award. He was the winner of Write About Now's Cookout Literary Prize. He has works published or forthcoming at *Strange Horizons*, *Ink Sweat & Tears*, *Augur Magazine*, *SAND Journal*, *MudRoom Mag*, *Bracken Magazine*, *The Shore Poetry*, *The Bitchin' Kitsch*, *The Deadlands*, *West Trade Review* and elsewhere. He is fond of his poorly lit room.

ARINZE CHIEMENAM
p. 87

Arinze Chiemenam is a graduate of English and Literary Studies from Chukwuemeka Odumegwu Ojukwu University. He is a young Nigerian poet, writer and storyteller who believes that literary works should promote humanity and reflect society. He believes that every human being deserves a voice and a chance, and most of his works consider the plight of the poor, the oppressed and the condemned. As a writer, he has had a short story published – 'Voices from the Slum' – and his works have been featured in several magazines, including in *BlazeVOX21*.

ABHAINN CONNOLLY
p. 123

Abhainn Connolly is a queer and trans poet that splits their time between the Pacific Northwest of the USA and Drogheda, Co. Louth, Ireland. Their work can be found in *Oxford Poetry*, *Poetry Ireland Review*, *HAD* and more. They made the longlist for Frontier Poetry's New Voices Contest 2022 and were a finalist for the 2021 Jack McCarthy Book Prize (Write Bloody). Their debut collection *DEADNAME* will be released in 2023.

JENNIFER COUSINS *p. 77*

Since retiring from a career as an international adoption and fostering specialist, Jennifer Cousins has volunteered as a therapeutic counsellor with newly arrived asylum seekers. She has been deeply affected by many of their stories. Jennifer has written a social-work column for the *Guardian*, won prizes for travel writing, has published books, journal articles and pieces on disability, adoption and fostering, and has had several flash-fiction pieces published. She has recently finished a novel about identity, adoption and displacement. Jennifer is the co-leader of a u3a creative writing group that focuses on flash and micro-fiction, humour and short poems.

MARTINS DEEP *p. 135*

Martins Deep is an Urhobo poet based in Zaria. He is a photographer and digital artist, and is currently a student at Ahmadu Bello University, Zaria. He has pieces published or forthcoming in *Magma Poetry*, *Strange Horizons*, *FIYAH*, *Augur Magazine*, *Lolwe*, *20.35 Africa*, *Fantasy Magazine*, *Josephine Quarterly*, *Anathema Magazine* and elsewhere. He doubles as a dreamer – fantasising reincarnating as an owl – and a sleepy workaholic.

KAT DIXON *p. 101*

Kat Dixon writes about relationships, social justice and queer identity. You can find her poetry in *The Rialto*, *Perverse*, *Butcher's Dog*, *Queerlings*, *Mslexia*, *fourteen poems* and *ReCreation Anthology*. She is a graduate of the MA in Writing Poetry with Newcastle University and The Poetry School. Alongside poetry, she is a digital-inclusion advocate and recently completed a research fellowship exploring ways to tackle Internet poverty.

ELLE ECHENDU *p. 83*

Elle Echendu is a high-school senior from Massachusetts. They run a magazine called *Blackademics*, where she discusses the Black community's contribution to academia.

DEBORAH FINDING *p. 81*

Deborah Finding is a queer feminist writer from the UK with a background in academia and activism. Her poetry has been published or is forthcoming in *fourteen poems*, *The Friday Poem*, *Ink Drinkers Poetry*, *Hearth & Coffin*, *Demos Rising* (Fly on the Wall), *Under Your Pillow* (Victorina) and *2022 Anthology* (Live Canon), and she was the winner of the Write By the Sea 2022 Poetry Competition. Other publications include interviews and features for *DIVA* magazine, the *Guardian* and the *Huffington Post*. She holds a PhD from LSE's Gender Institute and has degrees in Philosophy and Theology from Cambridge. Originally from the North-East, Deborah now lives in London.

ANITA GOVEAS *p. 115*

Anita Goveas is British-Asian, London-based and fuelled by strong coffee and paneer jalfrezi. She was first published in the *London Short Story Prize Anthology 2016*, and most recently by *West Trestle Review*. She's on the editorial team at FlashBack Fiction, teaches flash-fiction workshops with Far-hana Khalique and her debut flash collection, *Families and Other Natural Disasters*, was published in 2020.

SUMAN GUJRAL *p. 109*

Suman Gujral's history as a child of refugees and immigrants underlies her practice. Her parents were forcibly displaced by the 1947 Partition of India. It was during her MA that she came to understand the ongoing impact of Partition on them and millions of others. The cycle of war and displacement, rooted in colonial action, which un-homed her parents, continues today. She feels that as an artist and poet, she's in a unique position to cast a light on these difficult subjects. She is fascinated by the human ability to survive and thrive in the aftermath of difficult times.

OZ HARDWICK
p. 55

Oz Hardwick is a European poet, occasional photographer, wannabe musician and accidental academic whose work has been widely published in international journals and anthologies. He has published eleven full collections and chapbooks, including *Learning to Have Lost*, which won the 2019 Rubery International Book Award for poetry, and most recently *A Census of Preconceptions*. Currently he is as excited as a teenager about debut album *Paradox Paradigm* by his international/interdimensional space-rock collective Space Druids. Working-class and autistic, Oz is now Professor of Creative Writing at Leeds Trinity University. Who'd have thought it?

ROISÍN HARKIN
p. 67

Roisín Harkin is a mother of four young children, originally from the Inishowen Peninsula in Co. Donegal, Ireland, and now living in Solihull, West Midlands. She is currently taking time out from her career in the corporate world to focus on raising her children, and, when not being asked for a snack, writing poetry.

ELLIE HERDA-GRIMWOOD   *p. 69*

Ellie Herda-Grimwood started writing bits and pieces in 2021 as a means of release and was lucky enough to be published, building confidence and inspiring her to continue on and off. She is a proud Hufflepuff who enjoys pizza, film music and her adorably edible baby niece. She also loves her beautiful wife of ten years, without whom she mightn't have survived thus far. She is incredibly grateful to Renard Press (specifically lovely Will) for the continued support, and she does not profess to be classy at writing biographies. She resides in London and the hearts of children everywhere.

PETER HILL   *p. 63*

Born in the village of Haydock, formerly in West Lancashire, Peter is the second eldest of four children born to working-class parents. His earliest influence came from an uncle who was a published poet and gifted artist in oils. After an eight-year hiatus, Peter began writing poetry again during the early part of 2021. He draws inspiration from people, life, events and all things related to being human and the human condition.

SAM HONEYBONE   *p. 93*

Sam Honeybone is an eighteen-year-old musician and poet from Doncaster, South Yorkshire. He is a first-year classics student at Jesus College, Oxford, and was inspired to write poetry having studied the works of Hart Crane for his A-level English coursework. He often writes about masculinity, the body and ideas of queer heritage, seeking to explore the ways in which identities of today communicate with those of antiquity. 'Mum's Heels' is his first published poem.

OVERCOMER IBITEYE   *p. 75*

Overcomer Ibiteye is a poet and writer from Nigeria. Her works have been published in anthologies and magazines including *Land Luck Review, Iskanchi* and others. She was a finalist in the 2021 African Writers Awards and the 2022 Calanthe Collective Prize. When she's not writing she's reading crime novels.

LJ IRETON   *p. 133*

LJ is a poet and bookseller from London. She has a first-class degree in English Language and Literature from the University of Liverpool, and was a songwriter before focusing on poetry. She is passionate about animal rights and raising OCD awareness. Her poems have been published by numerous journals, including *Green Ink Poetry, The Madrigal, Noctivagant Press, Spellbinder Magazine, Drawn to the Light Press, Acropolis Journal, Mausoleum Press* and *Cerasus Magazine*.

TIM KIELY   *p. 107*

Tim Kiely is a criminal barrister and poet based in London. His work has been published in a number of outlets, including Fly on the Wall, *Under the Radar, South Bank Poetry* and *Magma*, and has appeared in anthologies from the Emma Press, the Ginkgo Prize for Ecopoetry and the Verve Poetry Festival Competition. His debut pamphlet, *Hymn to the Smoke*, was a winner of the 2020 Indigo Dreams First Pamphlet Competition.

MATT LEONARD *p. 117*

Matt Leonard is a practitioner psychologist, with a particular interest in supporting LGBTQ+ youth. Being a LGBTQ+ youth himself once (albeit a long time ago), his poetry builds on his own experiences and the intersectionality of identity.

NAOMI MADLOCK *p. 119*

Naomi Madlock is an exhausted poet and private tutor from Bristol. Her work has appeared in *Razz, UEA MA Poetry Anthology* and *Agapanthus Collective*. At the University of Exeter, she won the Gamini Salgado Prize for her dissertation titled *She Writes in Golden Ink: A Hive of Poems Celebrating the Femininity of the Honeybee*. She has a healthy obsession with dead things, which she collects in the cabinet of curiosities above her writing desk.

JAZZ MCCOULL *p. 71*

Jazz McCoull is a Yorkshire-born writer of prose and poetry, with a lifelong love of science fiction and an unapologetic punk worldview. Their work primarily deals with themes of identity and belonging (or a lack thereof), as related to gender and place.

DIANNE MCPHELIM *p. 31*

Born in Australia, Dianne McPhelim now lives in rural Ireland. Following various careers, she returned to college in 2020 to undertake a degree in Creative Writing and Literature. A winner of *The Sligo Weekender* short story competition, she has contributed history and heritage-themed articles to various Irish publications. She is currently working on a collection of short stories, and only recently began writing poetry.

JENNY MITCHELL   *p. 39*

Jenny Mitchell is a winner of the Poetry Book Awards 2021 and joint winner of the Geoff Stevens Memorial Prize 2019. Her poems have been widely published and have won numerous competitions, most recently the inaugural Ironbridge Prize 2022. Her debut collection, *Her Lost Language,* is one of 44 Poetry Books for 2019 (Poetry Wales). Her second collection, *Map of a Plantation,* is an *Irish Independent* 'Literary Find'. Both books are on the syllabus of Manchester Metropolitan University. Her third collection, *Resurrection of a Black Man*, is published in 2022.

RAINA MURIITHI   *p. 131*

Raina Muriithi is a young adult who writes about the unheard black experience. She grew up in Cambridgeshire for most of her life, apart from six years spent living in Tanzania. She is fluent in both English and Swahili. In her free time she knits, watches rom-coms and writes poetry about being Black and middle class and about the beauty of being Black and British. She has Kenyan heritage, of which she is extremely proud and passionate. Her favourite authors include Chimamanda Ngozi Adichie and Sophie Kinsella.

NESHMA   *49*

Neshma is an aspiring writer and film director. She is ethnically Assyrian Iraqi, grew up in Germany and lives in London. Her creative work explores themes of cultural identity, language and grief.

CAROLANN NORTH   *p. 105*

Carolann North is a poet, editor and researcher from Belfast, Northern Ireland. Her work has been published by Poetry Jukebox, *The Bangor Literary Journal* and *Wine Cellar Press*, among others. She has performed internationally, and has been funded by ACNI and the University of Atypical. In 2021, she won the ninth Bangor Poetry Competition for her poem 'Nesting'. She is the curator of Books Beyond Boundaries NI, an Ulster University project increasing diversity in speculative literature on the island of Ireland. She lives with her long-suffering daughter, two insufferable cats and more books than is appropriate, even for her.

JESSICA OAKWOOD   *p. 127*

Jessica Oakwood is a rainbow-haired neurodivergent non-binary sober mentally ill writer from the south-west of England. They have an undergraduate degree in English Literature and an MA in Creative Writing. They are autistic, dyslexic, on the waiting list for an ADHD assessment and have schizoaffective disorder. They are a self-described creative hurricane and fruit loop.

EWA GERALD ONYEBUCHI   *p. 25*

Ewa Gerald Onyebuchi is a Nigerian writer of Igbo descent. His writings – short stories and poems – aim at addressing topics related to the body, sexuality and feminism, with Africa as the focal point. An alumnus of Osiri University 2021 Creative Writing Masterclass taught by Professor Chigozie Obioma, he was shortlisted in 2020 for the Ibua Continental Call, was a finalist for the Spring

2021 Starlight Award for Poetry and was longlisted for the 2022 AUB International Poetry Prize.

CHIWENITE ONYEKWELU   *p. 103*

Chiwenite Onyekwelu is Nigerian, and is light-hearted. His poems have appeared in *The Adroit Journal*, *Chestnut Review*, *America Magazine*, *Gutter Magazine*, Rough Cut and elsewhere. He was a runner-up for the 2022 Foley Poetry Prize, finalist for the Gregory Djanikian Scholars in Poetry 2022, finalist for the New York Encounter Poetry Contest 2021 and winner of the Jack Grapes Poetry Prize 2020. He serves as Chief Editor at the School of Pharmacy Agulu, where he's an undergraduate.

IVY RAFF   *p. 23*

Ivy Raff is a co-founder of Make Your Medicine, a small collective of changemakers who support culture shifts at diverse workplaces. Her poetry has appeared in *The American Journal of Poetry*, *Nimrod International Journal* and *West Trade Review*, among several others. A current nominee for the *Best of the Net Anthology* and finalist for *Atlanta Review*'s International Poetry Contest, Ivy has been awarded residencies at Atlantic Center for the Arts and Alaska State Parks. Her work has received scholarship support from the Colgate Writers' Conference. She's studied Zen Buddhist approaches to writing under Natalie Goldberg and Subhana Barzaghi.

CAMERON REW   *p. 61*

Cameron Rew has moved back home to Liverpool after working as cabin crew for British Airways during his twenties. During worldwide travel, he loved witnessing the undulations of different cultures, drawing from this in their poetry. He studied an English Literature and 'Imaginative' Writing degree at Liverpool John Moores University from 2006, a course that took a slightly different approach, involving the instruction of Tai Chi, which they still practice, though not as often as he would like. He is currently enrolled on the Creative Writing MA at the University of Manchester, focusing on poetry.

MIA JASMINE RHODES   p. 21

Mia Jasmine Rhodes, also known as Ginger, is a nineteen-year-old writer, poet, aspiring surrealist filmmaker and Art History student. She can often be found reading novels with unlikeable female protagonists or in the surrealism section of an art gallery. She lived in Sydney, Australia during her childhood, and currently resides in West London. She hopes to pursue a Masters and PhD in Art History and Film and become a director.

KERRY RYAN   p. 139

Kerry Ryan lives in Folkestone in a house she loves with views of the English Channel. She writes poetry, plays and prose and is the contributing editor of *So Long as You Write*. Her writing has been featured in various publications including *Queerlings*, *The Manchester Review*, *the Kenyon Review*, *Spilling Ink* and others. Her play *Trust* was performed at the Gulbenkian Theatre. She is the founder of Write like a Grrrl, and her courses have been taught all over the world. She is passionate about access to the arts and utilising the arts to boost self-compassion and confidence.

DAPHNE SAMPSON   *p. 41*

Daphne Sampson was born in north London in 1950, and she started reading poetry as a moon-struck teenager. After growing up in Kent she worked in two wonderfully creative primary schools off the Old Kent Road, previously only known to her as that brown Monopoly card. This vibrant community had some of the exhilaration of the first plunge of a wild swim. She taught for two years in Kenya, which nourished her love of the natural world. Later, in Norfolk, with her young family, Daphne became involved in environmental campaigning. She had a severe stroke in 2020.

NNADI SAMUEL   *p. 97*

Nnadi Samuel holds a BA in English and Literature from the University of Benin. His micro-chapbook *Nature Knows a Little About Slave Trade* will be published in 2023. Nnadi has three times been named Best of the Net, and is a Pushcart Prize nominee, winner of the Canadian Open Drawer Contest 2020, International Human Right Arts Festival Award (IHRAF) New York 2021 and Angela C. Mankiewicz Poetry Contest.

LANA SILVER   *p. 27*

Lana Silver is originally from London, but fell in love with Wales, and now lives in Cardiff with her other half and their pets ('the fellas'). She has been writing and performing poetry since she was eight. Since then, she has been featured in anthologies with the Barbican Young Poets, Boscombe Revolution and Secret Chords from the Folklore Poetry Prize. Her work was recently commended in the New Voices

First Pamphlet Competition 2021. She is currently working on her first collection and is secretly enjoying the essays (and all the coffee) in her English Literature degree.

JESS SKYLESON   *p. 57*

Jess Skyleson is a queer, autistic former aerospace engineer who began writing poetry after being diagnosed with stage-four cancer at the age of thirty-nine. Currently in remission, they're now exploring new worlds in creative writing, with particular interests in Narrative Medicine, digital/sound poetry and early Zen Buddhist poems. They were awarded the 2022 International Hippocrates Poetry and Medicine Prize, received an honourable mention in the Tor House Poetry Prize and were a finalist for the Yemassee Poetry Prize and Kalanithi Writing Award. Their work has appeared in a number of literary journals and anthologies in both the US and the UK.

THEA SMILEY   *p. 45*

Thea Smiley is a poet and playwright from Suffolk. Her poetry has been shortlisted for the Bridport Prize and the Live Canon Collection competition 2022, longlisted by Gillian Clarke for the Rialto Nature and Place competition, and published in magazines, including *Spelt*, *The Alchemy Spoon* and *Ink Sweat & Tears*.

ALYSON SMITH   *p. 37*

Alyson Smith is based in Newcastle upon Tyne, and works as a writer and a visual artist. Alyson often considers her-self unable to fit into 'normal' society due to her diagnosis of bi-polar; however, her poetry has shown her just how reassuringly mundane her life actually is. She is currently in the second year of her MA in Creative Writing with the Open University.

FADAIRO TESLEEM   *p. 79*

Fadairo Tesleem is a Nigeria poet who writes from Ilorin, Kwara State. Tesleem is an alumnus of the Olongo Africa Poetry workshop and a member of the Hilltop Arts Foundation in Kwara. His poems are published or forthcoming in *Fiery Scribe Review*, *Arts Lounge Magazine*, *Blue Minaret*, *Down in the Dirt*, *Ninshär Arts*, *Blue paper*, *Upwrite Magazine*, *Inverse Journal*, *Second Chance Lit*, *Tilted House* and more.

SOPHIE LAURA WATERS   *p. 33*

Sophie is a trans femme poet and essayist based in Cambridge and London. She hatched in 2021. She loves partying and reading and is a bit of a polymath, writing about literature, world history, ethics, being trans and other universal themes. Her cat is the best cat it is possible to be.

OZZY WELCH   *p. 111*

Ozzy Welch is a student at King Edward VI College at Stourbridge, and rediscovered a love of poetry through their English Literature A-level. Their poetry explores queer culture, intimacy and the blurred lines found in the relationships they experience, underpinned by teenage morbidity.

FRANKIE WHITING   *p. 73*

Frankie will be twenty-four by the time this book is published, which is one year from twenty-five, which is halfway to fifty. Whilst they mainly write poetry, they do write both fiction and script on occasion. Frankie has been published in *Popshot Magazine* and *The Bolton Review*, which they later sub-edited and edited for. They never know what to write for these things and are always scared of coming across as arrogant. You will generally find Frankie with a plushie of a vegetable or food item in their dungarees.

DAVE WYNNE-JONES   *p. 141*

Dave Wynne-Jones has an MA in Creative Writing, taught poetry for twenty years, has climbed all the 4,000-metre mountains of the Alps and has had two non-fiction books on mountaineering published, as well as *Kidstuff*, a collection of poetry for children. *The Way Taken*, a poetry pamphlet based on an expedition to China, will be published in 2022. Covid and the ongoing Climate Crisis has been taking his work in more political directions.

DAMON YOUNG   *p. 59*

Damon Young is a winner of the Alzheimer's Society Poetry Prize. He has also been shortlisted for the Wells Festival of Literature Poetry Prize, The Robert Graves Poetry Prize, The Brian Dempsey Memorial Poetry Prize, The Canterbury Festival Poet of the Year and The Welshpool Poetry Prize. His first short collection *Family Room* was published in 2020.

LUCY ZHANG   *p. 121*

Lucy Zhang writes, codes and watches anime. Her work has appeared in *The Molotov Cocktail, Interzone, Hayden's Ferry Review* and elsewhere. She has had two chapbooks published in 2022, *Hollowed* and *Absorption*.

SUPPORTERS

This project was made possible through the financial support of the kind people listed below (in alphabetical order).

Jacqueline Bates
Chris and Joanna Cooke
Our Debbie
Deborah Finding
John Grieve
Ellie Herda-Grimwood
Samuel Honeybone
Clementine Koenig
Myiah Leite da Cunha Stevens
Matt Leonard
George Lowden
Raina Muriithi
David Panther
Petar Penda
Damon Young

And Anonymous, *on behalf of*
Auntie Lily, the Grimshaw girls and their brother Tom